At home with
Café 21

Classic cooking, social
surroundings, effortlessly right.

Café 21, 1 Trinity Gardens, Quayside, Newcastle NE1 2HH
0191 222 0755
www.cafetwentyone.co.uk

CHAMPAGNE
HENRIO

It's showtime. Sleek, social and seriously good food. Café 21 is bursting with city centre buzz and a culinary reputation to match.

This isn't the stuff of sober suits and formality though. Style may be sharp but the mood is relaxed. The vibe is easy and unhurried; linger on a stool by the bar, drink a cocktail, browse the menu and anticipate.

You know the food will be right. Ingredients treated with respect and imagination; the best produce speaks for itself. Satisfaction.

Cooking is about nourishment, pleasure and sometimes surprises. Often the greatest pleasure is the company around the table. The food can be simple but the people make the difference.

That's especially true when you cook at home, so we hope this collection of recipes from Café 21 will inspire you to gather friends, challenge yourself with new dishes and re-discover old favourites.

Food is an influence throughout life as these key players in the Café 21 team reveal.

Terry Laybourne

Bastiaan Hogelucht, general manager, Café 21

I am Dutch so obviously chips and mayonnaise have featured heavily in my culinary upbringing. Another dish I remember well is Dutch pea soup, as exciting as it sounds! I never go home without trying some Indonesian food; there is a great choice in Holland and it is superb.

As a home cook I like preparing fish and I cook pasta dishes – I don't spend more than half an hour in the kitchen though.

Chris Dobson, head chef, Café 21

When I was a kid we had an allotment so we were always out there picking fresh vegetables and fruit. My dad would bring home a whole fish and clean and prep it in the kitchen sink. I would stand and watch, wanting to have a go myself. He did all the cooking - fantastic fruit crumbles. My seven-year-old loves helping me in the kitchen.

Even now I'd say roast chicken is my favourite. I always sit down to a roast on a Sunday.

THE RECIPES

Starters

Main Courses

Desserts

XANADU

EXMOOR DRIVE

2007 CABERNET SAUVIGNON

Starters

Beetroot Salad

Cheddar Cheese and Spinach Soufflé

Rare Salmon Spring Rolls with Soy-citrus Dipping Sauce

Crab Lasagne with Shellfish Cappuccino

Steak Tartare

Beetroot Salad

Serves 6

Try your best to find the different varieties of beets for this salad; they give a stunning visual effect, as well as tasting so good. Alternatively, why not think about growing your own?

Beets
1 large handful Rock salt
8 mixed Beets (red, pink, golden and candy striped)
250ml Cabernet Sauvignon wine vinegar
250g Caster sugar

Mustard vinaigrette
3tbls White wine vinegar
50g Caster sugar
1tbls Dijon mustard
4tbls Sour cream

Salad
1 small handful Lambs lettuce
2tbls Mustard vinaigrette (above)
6 Softish boiled eggs (9 minutes)
50g Piece of fresh horseradish
Maldon sea salt
Freshly milled white pepper

1   Sit the beetroots on a bed of rock salt and bake in the oven at 160°C for an hour or so until they are tender
2   Allow to cool then peel away the skins
3   Cut the flesh into a variety of shapes and sizes (keeping the different beetroots apart from one another)
4   Dissolve 250g of the sugar in the red wine vinegar and divide between four dishes
5   Drop each type of beetroot into a separate bowl, set aside and toss occasionally
6   Whisk sugar with the white wine vinegar. Add the mustard then the sour cream and season

Assembly
1   Dress the lambs lettuce with the vinaigrette and scatter between four plates
2   Tumble the different beetroots over and around the plate
3   Halve the eggs and arrange on the salad, seasoning the yolk with a little Maldon sea salt and a grind of pepper
4   Spoon the mustard dressing over then grate a little fresh horseradish on top
5   Serve immediately

Cheddar Cheese and Spinach Soufflé

Serves 4

In the same way that you'd be seriously disappointed if you went to a Rolling Stones concert and they didn't play Jumping Jack Flash, a Café 21 menu without this soufflé is almost unthinkable!

50g Unsalted butter
4tbls Fine dry white breadcrumbs
80ml Full fat milk
¼ Onion
1 small Bay leaf
1 Clove
30g Plain flour
1tsp English mustard powder
60g Spinach
150g Mature Cheddar cheese
3 small Eggs
Salt
Freshly milled white pepper
400ml Double cream

1   Butter four 3½" ramekins using a small pastry brush then line each with a layer of dry breadcrumbs. Chill in the refrigerator

2   Pre-heat the oven to 135°C

3   Separate the eggs

4   Heat the milk in a saucepan with onion studded with clove and bay leaf

5   Remove from heat, cover with a lid and allow to infuse

6   Make a roux by melting 30g butter in another saucepan and stirring in the flour. Cook over a low heat for five minutes

7   Stir in English mustard powder

8   Strain and reheat the milk, then add to the roux, one ladle at a time, stirring well and allowing to almost boil between each addition

9   When all of the milk has been added and the mixture is smooth, move to a low heat and allow to cook out gently for 15-20mins, stirring regularly

10 Remove from the heat and stir in the egg yolks and 100g grated Cheddar cheese, then cover the pan with cling film to retain heat

11 Heat remaining 10g butter until 'nut brown' in a non-stick frying pan and sauté spinach very briefly until it has wilted

12 Season the spinach with salt and pepper then drain in a colander

13 Transfer the spinach to a cutting board, chop coarsely with a large knife then stir into the cheese sauce

14 Whisk the egg whites until they begin to thicken, adding a tiny pinch of salt

15 Continue whisking until quite firm (beware of graining and drying out)

16 Beat a third of the whites into the cheese sauce with a wooden spoon then fold in the remainder very carefully using a rubber spatula

17 Divide the mixture evenly between prepared soufflé moulds and sit the moulds in a tray of hot water. Transfer to the oven and bake for 25 minutes

18 Remove the tray from the oven and allow to cool for 5 minutes, increase oven to 200°C

19 Turn out the soufflés into four individual buttered oven-proof dishes and pour the double cream equally between them. Scatter the remaining grated cheese over

20 Return to the oven and bake for another 12 minutes or so until almost doubled in size and golden on top

21 Serve immediately

Rare Salmon Spring Rolls with Soy-citrus Dipping Sauce

Serves 4

You'll need a visit to the Asian supermarket before embarking on this recipe. Make more rolls if you wish as they freeze well and are perfect deep-fried straight from the freezer. Just cook them for an extra minute or so, and then leave to rest for a further two minutes before serving.

400g piece Salmon fillet (centre cut)
1tbls Wasabi paste
2tbls Coarsely chopped coriander leaves
2tbls Coarsely chopped flat parsley
12 Spring roll wrappers
Egg white
8 Coriander sprigs

1   Cut the salmon into 12 fingers approximately 85mm long x 15mm x 15mm
2   Brush each lightly with wasabi
3   Mix chopped coriander and parsley together and roll the salmon fingers, coating them on all sides
4   Wrap each finger in a spring roll wrapper, using a little egg white to seal ends
5   Deep fry in oil heated to 190°C for 30-45 seconds until lightly golden (the salmon should be hot on the outside but still very rare in the centre
6   Drain on kitchen paper
7   Serve dipping sauce on the side and garnish with coriander sprigs

Soy-citrus dressing

3tsp Wasabi powder
6tbls Kikomann soy sauce
4tbls Mirin
2tbls Mustard oil
2tbls Lime juice
2tsp Honey
Freshly milled black pepper

1   Place wasabi powder into a bowl and mix until smooth with a little soy sauce
2   Add the remaining ingredients and whisk together to serve

Crab Lasagne with Shellfish Cappuccino

Serves 6

6 Lasagne sheets
190g Scallop meat without roe
250ml Double cream
1 Egg yolk
500g White crabmeat
½ bunch Basil leaves (reserve stalks for the sauce)
Salt and cayenne pepper
300ml Shellfish sauce*

1. Bring a large pan of salted water to a boil and cook the lasagne sheets for 8 minutes then refresh under cold running water. Drain and dry on a clean tea towel

2. Cut the sheets into 18 x 65mm discs using a pastry cutter. Store on tray between two sheets of cling film to prevent drying

3. Chill the scallops, double cream and egg yolk

4. Blend the scallops in a liquidiser with a large pinch of salt and small pinch of cayenne pepper. Then add the egg yolk and the double cream

5. Transfer the mixture to a bowl over ice and fold in the crab meat and the chopped basil

6. Butter 6 x 65mm stainless steel rings and place on a tray lined with baking parchment

7. Place a disc of pasta in the base of each ring, then a spoonful of the crab mixture, followed by another disc of pasta and another spoon of crab mixture

8. Top with a final disc of pasta and steam the parcels for 11 minutes

9. Transfer carefully to individual bowls before removing the stainless steel rings

10. Reheat the shellfish sauce and create a foam using a hand blender before spooning over the lasagne

11. Shred the basil leaves and scatter a pinch over each lasagne parcel

*Shellfish sauce

50ml Olive oil
400g Prawns in shell
50g Butter
½ small Onion
½ Carrot
½ Celery stick
⅛ Fennel bulb
2 Garlic cloves
8 Coriander seeds
1 point from Star anise
3 ripe Tomatoes (chopped)
½tbls Tomato paste
1tbls Cognac
1 glass White wine
Water
Basil stalks
200ml Double cream
¼ Lemon

1. Peel the vegetables and chop finely. Sweat slowly in butter with the garlic, coriander seeds and star anise

2. When softened add the tomato paste and tomatoes. Continue cooking until the moisture has evaporated

3. Heat the olive oil in a frying pan until almost smoking and fry the prawns for a minute or so until very aromatic, then drain in a colander before adding to the saucepan with the vegetables

4. Deglaze with cognac and then the white wine. Boil to reduce by two thirds then add enough water to just cover the prawns

5. Simmer for 1 hour, then liquidise and pass through a fine sieve into a clean saucepan, add the basil stalks and leave to infuse for 20 minutes then strain

6. Bring back to a boil and simmer until reduced to 200ml then add the double cream and simmer to a sauce consistency

7. Check seasoning and sharpen with a squeeze of lemon

Steak Tartare

Serves 4

Serve as a first course or increase quantities and serve with thin cut chips and a green salad for a main course.

1 Egg yolk
1½tbls Dijon mustard
1½tbls Tomato ketchup
¾tsp Worcestershire sauce
¾tsp Tabasco sauce
1 splash Cognac
4 Chopped cocktail gherkins
3tbls Chopped red onion
1tbls Fine capers (rinsed)
½tsp Chopped chives
½tsp Chopped tarragon
1tbls Chopped flat parsley
1 Anchovy fillet, chopped
450g Tail end of beef fillet (or sirloin steak), well chilled
Maldon sea salt
Freshly milled black pepper
4 Quails eggs (separated)
Hot toast

1   Combine the egg yolk, mustard, ketchup, Worcestershire sauce, Tabasco and Cognac in a chilled glass bowl. Mix well with a table fork

2   Then add the finely chopped onion, gherkins, capers, herbs and the chopped anchovy fillet

3   Remove the beef from the refrigerator and trim away any fat or gristle then slice with a very sharp knife into 3mm slices. Stack the slices then cut across the stack every 3mm. Turn the meat and cut into 3mm dice

4   Transfer to a bowl and place this within a larger bowl filled with ice

5   Add the sauce mixture to the meat a little at a time, mixing gently with a table fork until just combined

6   Season well with sea salt and freshly milled black pepper

7   Test a little for seasoning and add salt, pepper or Tabasco as required (the tartare should be quite highly seasoned and have a little kick from the Tabasco)

8   Mould onto four individual plates and top each with a quails egg yolk*

9   Serve with an ample amount of hot toast

*Serve the quail's egg yolk in its shell. The shell should be pierced with a knifepoint and can then easily be halved with a knife or scissors. Separate the yolk from the white then replace it back in the shell and on top of the steak tartare.

Main Courses

Roasted Rump of Northumbrian Lamb with Fine Beans and Tomatoes

Medallions of Northumbrian Venison with Red Wine Cherries

Pan-roasted Cod Fillet with Chorizo and Cannellini Beans

Cassoulet

Fillet of Turbot with Spring Vegetables and Truffle

Roasted Rump of Northumbrian Lamb with Fine Beans and Tomatoes

Serves 4

---

4 Lamb rumps
80ml Extra virgin olive oil
1 sprig Bay
½ small bunch Rosemary
½ small bunch Thyme
Maldon sea salt
Freshly milled black pepper
175ml Lamb gravy

1   Season the lamb with sea salt and black pepper then drizzle with oil
2   Gather the herbs into a bundle and rub vigorously over the lamb
3   Sear in a heavy cast iron frying pan then transfer to the oven at 180°C for around 12 minutes with the herbs on top (turning and basting every few minutes)
4   Remove from the pan and rest for 15 minutes whilst preparing the beans

Beans

265g Extra fine beans
40ml Extra virgin olive oil
8 Cherry tomatoes
3 Garlic cloves (peeled and very finely sliced)
1½tbls Fine capers
2tbls Sliced small black olives

1   Cook the beans in lots of boiling salted water until tender then refresh in iced water – drain in a colander
2   Heat the olive oil in a frying pan over a medium heat
3   Add tomatoes and garlic, cook for 2-3 minutes until softened
4   Stir in beans, capers, olives and lamb gravy, bringing briefly to a simmer

Medallions of Northumbrian Venison with Red Wine Cherries
Serves 4

At Café 21 we serve this venison dish with braised Savoy cabbage and spätzle but it works equally well with croquette potatoes or noodles and red or spring cabbage.

700g Boneless roe deer saddle
Salt
Freshly milled black pepper
2tbls Vegetable oil
30g Unsalted butter
250g Cherries
75g Caster sugar
125ml Balsamic vinegar
250ml Red wine
¼ Cinnamon stick
160g Butternut squash puree

1   Stone the cherries
2   Warm the sugar in a small saucepan until melted
3   Add the wine, balsamic vinegar and cinnamon, bring to a boil to reduce a little then add cherries
4   Simmer gently until the cherries are tender and nicely glazed
5   Cut the venison into 8 x 85g medallions and flatten slightly with a steak mallet
6   Heat 2 large frying pans over a high heat with 1tbls of vegetable oil in each
7   Add the venison medallions, a knob of butter and cook for 2 minutes before turning and cooking for a further minute on the second side
8   Remove the pan from the heat and transfer the venison to a small tray to keep warm
9   Divide the squash puree between 4 warm plates
10 Arrange the venison medallions alongside, then spoon the cherries and their sauce over and around

Butternut Squash Puree

400g Butternut squash
50ml Full fat milk
20g Unsalted butter
5ml Hazelnut oil

1   Peel and deseed the squash and cut into 4cms pieces
2   Cook for about 8-10 minutes in lots of boiling salted water until very soft
3   Drain and press well in a cloth to remove any excess liquid
4   Transfer to a liquidiser and process until very smooth
5   Bring milk to a boil and add to the squash puree in the liquidiser, adding butter and hazelnut oil. Check seasoning and serve

Pan-roasted Cod Fillet with Chorizo and Cannellini Beans
Serves 4

4 x 160g Cod fillets
10ml Extra virgin olive oil
200g Chorizo, thin links
Fine sea salt
Freshly milled white pepper
1 Egg yolk, whisked
250g Floury potatoes
180g Canned cannellini beans, drained and rinsed
55ml Sherry vinegar
80g Unsalted butter
280ml Chicken stock
Basil leaves
Sherry butter sauce*

1   Peel the potatoes and cut into even sized chunks. Cook in boiling salted water then drain in a colander. Return the potatoes to the pan, cover with a lid and place over a medium heat for 3-4 minutes to steam dry. Add 140g of the cannellini beans to the pan and crush together with a fork whilst everything is hot

2   Beat in the boiling chicken stock, then the butter and sherry vinegar

3   Season with salt and pepper, cover and keep warm whilst you prepare the fish

4   Remove the skin from the cod fillets if necessary

5   Cut the chorizo into thin rounds with a very sharp knife. Season the cod, then brush the skin side with a little egg yolk and arrange overlapping slices of chorizo in the form of scales

6   Gently pan fry on the chorizo covered side for two minutes with a little olive oil in a non-stick frying pan. Turn and cook for a further 5-6 minutes, depending on the thickness of the fish. Remove from the pan and drain on kitchen paper

7   Transfer the cod fillets to warm plates, spoon the crushed potatoes mixture alongside

8   Reheat the sauce with the remaining cannellini beans and spoon around the fish with chopped basil leaves

*Sherry Butter Sauce

100g Butter
125ml Chicken stock
½tsp Cream
25ml Sherry vinegar
Maldon sea salt
Freshly milled black pepper

1   Heat the butter in a small saucepan until the foam subsides and the butter turns nut brown. Pour immediately into a bowl, sitting in a bowl of iced water and whisk the butter until it begins to thicken. Pour onto a small plate, cover with cling film and refrigerate

2   Bring the chicken stock to a boil in a small saucepan and simmer to reduce by half

3   Remove the browned butter from the fridge and cut into small cubes

4   Add the cream to the chicken stock then whisk in the browned butter a little at a time

5   Flavour with sherry vinegar to taste and season with salt and pepper

6   Keep warm until needed

Cassoulet

Serves 4

A standard-bearer for French provincial cookery the Cassoulet's origins are in the South West. As is often the case there are three 'original' versions with Toulouse, Carcassonne and Castelnaudary all claiming their version to be the real 'I am'.

400g Dried haricot beans, soaked overnight in cold water

1 Carrot, peeled

2 small Onions, peeled

1 Clove

4 Garlic cloves, peeled and crushed

100g Pork rind

1 Bouquet garni

1 Toulouse sausage

1 Garlic sausage

100g Pork belly

1 Confit duck leg, cut into 4 pieces

2tbls Duck fat or lard

320g Lamb shoulder, cut into 40g dice

1 Plum tomato, peeled and chopped

2tbls Breadcrumbs

1tbls Chopped flat leaf parsley

Salt

Freshly milled black pepper

1. Drain the beans and rinse with fresh water

2. Put them into a large pan with the carrot, 1 onion studded with the clove, 2 garlic cloves, pork rind and bouquet garni

3. Cover generously with cold water and place over a high heat

4. Lower the heat before it boils, skim and simmer very gently for an hour

5. Add the sausages and simmer for another 15 minutes before removing the pan from the heat and seasoning with salt and pepper

6. Place the pork belly in a large pan, cover with cold water and bring to a simmer - cook for 5 minutes then refresh under cold running water, drain and cut into 4 thick slices

7. Melt the duck fat in a heavy saucepan, season the diced lamb and brown on all sides - remove with a slotted spoon and drain on kitchen paper

8. Slice the remaining onion, add to the same frying pan and sauté for 3 minutes before adding the tomato, the remaining garlic and 60ml of the bean cooking liquid. Simmer for 10 minutes

9. Lift the pork rind, sausages, onions and bouquet garni from the bean pot. Drain the beans in a colander, retaining the liquid

10. Add the beans to the pan with the sliced onions

11. Slice the garlic sausage into 1cms thick rounds and cut the Toulouse sausage into 4 chunks

12. Lay the pork rind in the base of a casserole and fill with alternating layers of bean mixture and meats (lamb, duck and sausage)

13. Finish with a layer of beans and drizzle with 1tbls of melted duck fat

14. Add enough retained bean cooking liquid to just reach the top layer of beans

15. Bake for 3 hours at 120°C, adding more liquid as it cooks

16. Mix the breadcrumbs with the parsley and scatter over the surface before returning to the oven for another half hour to brown

17. Place the casserole in the centre of the table with a bowl of dressed green salad and lots of crusty bread

Fillet of Turbot with Spring Vegetables and Truffle

Serves 6

30g Parma ham
3 Spring onions
250ml Chicken stock
Maldon sea salt
Freshly milled white pepper
1½kg Fresh peas in the pod
400g Fresh broad beans
80g Unsalted butter
80g Whole skinned almonds
3tbls Black truffle paste
1tsp Black truffle oil
6 x 170g Turbot fillets
1tbls Sunflower oil
1 Lemon

1. Pop the peas and broad beans from their pods then remove the fine skin from the broad beans. You should now have around 400g shelled peas and 125g broad beans

2. Cut the ham into fine strips about 1"long and the spring onions into 4mm thick rounds

3. Sweat them together with ½tbls butter in a small saucepan. Add the chicken stock, bring to a boil and set aside

4. Cook the broad beans and 100g of peas in boiling salted water until just tender then refresh in iced water

5. In another pan of boiling salted water, cook the remaining peas until very soft, drain then transfer to a liquidiser and blend until smooth, adding 1tbls butter. Season with salt, pepper and a pinch of sugar. Keep warm

6. Bring another pan of water to the boil and blanch the almonds for 3 minutes, then drain

7. Season the turbot fillets with salt and pepper and pan fry for 3 minutes on each side in a non-stick frying pan with 1tbls of vegetable oil. Finish with a little squeeze of lemon then remove to a plate and keep warm

8. Bring the pan with the ham and chicken stock back to a boil then whisk in 4tbls of cold butter a little at a time to create a light glossy emulsion (it shouldn't become too heavy or rich) next whisk in the truffle oil, truffle paste, the reserved peas, broad beans and almonds. Check for seasoning and adjust if necessary. Finish with a tiny squeeze of lemon

9. Divide the pea puree between 6 warm plates, top with a turbot fillet then spoon the truffle and vegetable sauce over

Desserts

Chilled Cherry Soup with Yoghurt Sorbet

Hot Chocolate Doughnut with Pistachio Ice Cream

Steamed Apple and Blackberry Pudding

Palet d'Or

Soft Meringue Roll with Rose Petal Cream and Strawberries

Chilled Cherry Soup with Yoghurt Sorbet

Serves 4

375g Fresh cherries
50ml Maraschino liquer
100g Sugar
8 Strawberries
8 Blackberries
8 Raspberries
12 Blueberries
4 scoops Yoghurt sorbet

1   Wash and stone the cherries. Place together with the sugar and Maraschino into a heat proof bowl, then cover tightly with cling film. Place the bowl over a pan of simmering water for 45 mins

2   Remove from the heat and leave to cool, leaving the cling film in place, then transfer to the fridge to chill

3   Wash and pick over the fruits, cut the strawberries into quarters and the blackberries in half, leave the blueberries and raspberries whole

4   Divide the fruits evenly between 4 chilled soup bowls and ladle the cherry soup over

5   Serve a scoop of yoghurt sorbet into the centre of each bowl

Yoghurt Sorbet

125ml Water
175g Caster sugar
25ml Liquid glucose
420g Natural yoghurt

1   Bring water, sugar and glucose to a rolling boil

2   Remove from the heat and allow to cool before whisking together with the yoghurt

3   Transfer into an ice cream machine and churn

Hot Chocolate Doughnut with Pistachio Ice Cream

Serves 4

This isn't quite your run-of-the-mill jam doughnut. It uses rich brioche dough packed with butter and the best quality dark chocolate. The result is a hot, crispy, light and unctuous mouthful... too good to be true!

Brioche dough

250g Plain flour
1 Egg yolk
3 Eggs
30g Caster sugar
5g Salt
12g Fresh yeast
200g Unsalted butter, softened

1. Combine flour, sugar, salt and yeast in the bowl of an electric mixer
2. Mix slowly using a dough hook attachment
3. Begin adding the butter a little at a time and mix until combined
4. Continue mixing until the dough leaves the sides of the bowl and becomes smooth and elastic
5. Transfer the dough to a clean bowl and cover with cling film
6. Refrigerate overnight to allow dough to prove

Ganache

100ml Double cream
100g Best quality dark chocolate (grated or broken into small pieces)

1. Bring cream to the boil and remove from heat
2. Add chocolate to the cream and mix until smooth
3. Cover with cling film and refrigerate for 3 hours
4. Transfer the ganache into a piping bag with a 1cms plain nozzle and pipe into four 6cms diameter rings on a sheet of non-stick baking parchment
5. Freeze

Assembly

1. Next day, divide the dough into two and roll out on a floured surface to approx 2-3 cms thick
2. Place the frozen chocolate rings on top of one of the sheets of dough, leaving enough space for the edges of the dough to be sealed
3. Brush a little water around the edge of each chocolate ring
4. Place the other sheet of dough on top and press down using your fingers. Create a hole in the dough with an apple corer
5. Cut out each doughnut using a 85mm round cutter and pinch the edges together carefully making sure to seal well, use a little flour to prevent sticking
6. Place on a clean sheet of silicone paper and refrigerate until needed

Cooking

1. Fill a deep saucepan three quarters full with vegetable oil and heat to 170°C
2. Place doughnuts into the hot oil, two at a time and cook until golden 3- 4 mins approx, turning once
3. Lift gently from the hot oil using a slotted spoon and drain well on kitchen paper
4. Then roll in a little caster sugar
5. Serve piping hot with pistachio ice cream

Steamed Apple and Blackberry Pudding
Serves 4

150g Sugar
3 Eggs
170g Soft unsalted butter
170g Self-raising flour
8g Baking powder
Finely grated zest and juice from 1 lemon
16 Blackberries
60g Apple compote

1 Sieve flour and baking powder together
2 Whisk eggs in a mixing machine
3 Warm sugar in oven then shower into the eggs and continue whisking until white and a 'ribbon' forms
4 Add butter in small pieces, a little at a time
5 Fold in the sifted flour then the grated lemon zest and juice
6 Butter and flour 4 individual pudding basins and place 4 blackberries in the base of each, followed by a tablespoon of apple compote
7 Fill, almost to the brim with sponge mixture and cover each loosely with a piece of buttered foil
8 Steam for 45 minutes then allow to rest for 5 minutes before turning out into dessert bowls
9 Serve with a jug of hot Crème Anglaise*

Apple compote

150g Butter
100g Sugar
1 Bramley apple

1 Peel and core the apple, cut into 1.5cms chunks
2 Melt the butter in a stainless steel saucepan then add the sugar
3 Allow sugar to melt before throwing in the diced apples
4 Allow to cook uncovered, stirring from time to time until the apples are soft
5 Remove from heat and allow to cool

*Crème Anglaise

6 Egg yolks
110g Caster sugar
500ml Full fat milk
1 Vanilla Pod split and seeds removed

1 Heat the milk with half of the sugar, the vanilla pod and seeds
2 Whisk the eggs yolks and remaining sugar in a bowl until white and thickened slightly
3 When the milk boils, pour half of it onto the yolks and mix until smooth then add this to the remaining milk in the pan
4 Return to a low heat and cook, stirring continuously with a wooden spoon, until the mixture thickens enough to coat the back of the spoon. Alternatively use a digital thermometer and cook to 82°C
5 Pour from the pan immediately into a clean bowl which is sitting inside another bowl filled with iced water
6 Remove the vanilla pod
7 Reheat by sitting the bowl over a pan of boiling water to warm

Palet d'Or

Serves 6

The recipe looks far more complicated than it really is. If you take a step-by-step approach, you'll actually find it all quite simple.

Salted Caramel

30g Vanilla sugar
1tsp Butter, softened
30ml Double cream
½tsp Liquid glucose
½tsp Maldon sea salt
25g Rice crispies
65g Milk chocolate

1 Heat sugar in a small saucepan over a medium heat until it dissolves and turns to a golden caramel. Stir gently with a wooden spoon
2 Very carefully add the double cream a little at a time (be careful as the mixture may spit and splatter)
3 Add glucose and salt and mix well
4 Remove from the heat and allow to cool
5 Melt the milk chocolate gently and stir into the salted caramel together with the rice crispies
6 Arrange 6 80mm x 15mm dessert rings on a tray lined with non stick baking parchment and spoon a little of the mixture into the base of each; flattening slightly with the back of the spoon. Refrigerate for 10 minutes to set the mixture

Chocolate Filling

55g Dark chocolate couverature (70% cocoa solids)
35g Unsalted butter
35g Caster sugar
15g Clear honey
1tbls Freshly made Espresso coffee
24g Cocoa powder
2 Egg yolks
65ml Double cream
1tsp Amaretto

1 Break the chocolate couverature into small pieces and place into a bowl
2 Bring the cream to a boil and pour over the chocolate. Stir until chocolate is fully melted and mixture is smooth. Set aside at room temperature

3 Cream the butter, sugar and honey until light and fluffy using the beater attachment in a small mixing machine
4 Gradually add the Amaretto and the espresso, followed quickly by the egg yolks and the cocoa powder
5 Quickly fold in the chocolate
6 Spoon into the prepared rings over the crunchy base, smoothing the tops with a palette knife
7 Transfer to deep freeze until needed

Chocolate Glaze

120ml Double cream
100g Dark chocolate (55% cocoa solids)

1 Break the chocolate into bite size pieces and place into a bowl
2 Bring the cream to a boil and pour directly over the chocolate
3 Stir gently until fully melted and smooth

Assembly

1 Sheet edible gold leaf
4 Chocolate curls

1 Remove the desserts from the freezer. Warm the ring moulds with your hands to allow the desserts to slide out easily
2 Place them on a cooling wire with a tray underneath
3 Coat with the chocolate glaze by ladling a generous amount over the top and allow to run off the sides
4 Lift from the wire using a palette knife and chill and set the glaze
5 Serve decorated with chocolate curls and a little edible gold leaf

Soft Meringue Roll with Rose Petal Cream and Strawberries

Serves 6

180g Egg whites
360g Sugar
20g Cornflour
10ml White wine vinegar
500ml Double cream
200g Rose petal jelly, softened
150g Icing sugar
1tbls Rosewater

1. Preheat the oven to 180°C
2. Whisk egg whites to a soft peak then gradually shower in the sugar whilst continuing to whisk to a stiff meringue
3. Whisk in the cornflour and the vinegar
4. Spread onto a 250 mm x 150mm Swiss roll tin, lined with non-stick baking parchment and bake in the preheated oven for 20 minutes
5. Remove and allow to cool before turning out onto another sheet of baking parchment
6. For the rosewater cream; whisk the double cream until it begins to thicken then sift in the icing sugar. Then gently fold in the rose petal jelly and flavour with rosewater to taste
7. Spread a generous layer of cream over the meringue and roll carefully with the help of the silicone paper – chill well

Strawberry and rosewater coulis

100g Strawberries, washed and hulled
1tsp Icing sugar
½tsp Rosewater

Liquidise the strawberries and icing sugar, then pass through a fine sieve into a bowl. Flavour to taste with rosewater

Assembly

250g Strawberries, washed, hulled and quartered
½tsp Chopped pistachio nuts (optional)
Icing sugar to dust
4 Sprigs mint

Cut the meringue roll into thick slices and serve topped with quartered strawberries and scattered pistachios with a little strawberry coulis

A restaurant is about far more than the dish delivered to the table. The 'backstage' team is invaluable and every role is as crucial as the next. They are, in food-speak, the vital ingredients... and as such well deserving of a heartfelt thank you:

Bastiaan Hogelucht, Steven Henderson, Karen Alexander, Tomasz Szymczykowski, Scott Paterson, Roy Ng, Alistair Kendall, Jennifer Burnett, Orla Forker, Jamie Oliver, Emilia Lapinska, Jessica Hall, Alexandra Veltze, Michaela Murphy- Collins, Carol Robinson, Amy Oliver, Eamonn Richardson, Sarah Brown, Kelly Steele, Laura Jobson , Chris Dobson, Clare Armstrong, Martin Malinowski-Evans, Chris Eagle, Helen Doyle, Darren Busby, Craig Dickinson, Steven Foister, Jonathan Cairns, Richard Wheatley, Claire Hodgson, Adam Mckeown, Agnieska Matysiek, Paul Hesson, Stefan Milligan, Marta Lada, Alfie Wilkinson, Emilia Demczuk, Esmeraldo Da Costa, Wojciech Gronkiewicz, Jose Fiaes, Beverley Fleck and Wojciech Matysiek.

Monday, 11.30am, pre-service.

At home with Café 21 is one of a set of four books featuring recipes from the restaurants of Terry Laybourne's 21 Hospitality Group.

Others in the series are:
At home with Caffè Vivo
At home with Café 21 at Fenwick
At home with Bistro 21

Copies available from the restaurants or to order.
Contact 0191 222 0755
www.cafetwentyone.co.uk
marketing@21hospitality.co.uk

Recipes: Chris Dobson, Clare Armstrong and Terry Laybourne
Design: Euan Underwood
Editor: Kathryn Armstrong
Photography: Kevin Gibson

Published by room501, Publishing House, 16 Pickersgill Court,
Quay West Business Park, Sunderland SR5 2AQ.
0191 537 5720
www.room501.co.uk

ISBN: 978-1-906916-01-5

A huge thank you to our very generous supporters,

www.planeta.it
www.rathbonewinegroup.com
www.montgras.cl
www.champagne-henriot.com
www.enotria.co.uk

... lovely people who make great wines.

At home with
Café 21